animals**animals**

Geese

by **Darice Bailer**

mc **Marshall Cavendish** Benchmark

New York

Special thanks to Donald E. Moore III, associate director of animal care at the Smithsonian Institution's National Zoo, for his expert reading of this manuscript.

Other Marshall Cavendish Offices:
Marshall Cavendish International (Asia) Private Limited, 1 New Industrial Road, Singapore 536196 • Marshall Cavendish International (Thailand) Co Ltd. 253 Asoke, 12th Flr, Sukhumvit 21 Road, Klongtoey Nua, Wattana, Bangkok 10110, Thailand • Marshall Cavendish (Malaysia) Sdn Bhd, Times Subang, Lot 46, Subang Hi-Tech Industrial Park, Batu Tiga, 40000 Shah Alam, Selangor Darul Ehsan, Malaysia

Marshall Cavendish is a trademark of Times Publishing Limited

All websites were available and accurate when this book was sent to press.

Library of Congress Cataloging-in-Publication Data
Bailer, Darice.
Geese / by Darice Bailer.
p. cm. — (Animals animals)
Includes index.
Summary: "Provides comprehensive information on the anatomy, special skills, habitats, and diet of geese"—Provided by publisher.
ISBN 978-0-7614-4840-2
1. Geese—Juvenile literature. I. Title.
QL696.A52B32 2011
598.4'17—dc22
2009019482

Front cover: The Greylag goose is a wild goose found in Europe, Asia, and the United States.

Photo research by Joan Meisel

Cover photo: imagebroker/Alamy

The photographs in this book are used by permission and through the courtesy of:
Alamy: blickwinkel, 11; Van Duncan/Kenebec Images, 12; Holger Elers, 13; David Tipling, 36; Mark A. Johnson, 39. *Corbis:* Julie Habel, 26. *Getty Images:* John Downer, 1; Thomas Kitchin & Victoria Hurst, 4; Pearl Bucknell, 6; DEA Picture Library, 8; Neal Michler, 10; Dominick Spolitino, 14; Derek P. Redfearn, 16; Tim Graham, 17, 20, 30, 33; Darrell Gulin, 18; Stephen Krasemann, 22; Martin Ruegner, 24; Michael S. Quinton, 25; Burazin, 28, 31; Johnny Johnson, 34, 41; altrendo nature, 40.

Editor: Joy Bean
Publisher: Michelle Bisson
Art Director: Anahid Hamparian
Series Designer: Adam Mietlowski

Printed in Malaysia (T)
1 3 5 6 4 2

Contents

1 Mates Forever

Seven geese gather on a patch of grass near a blue-gray ocean. They are a family of Canada geese—two parents and their five fuzzy babies, or *goslings*. The adults have black bills, dark brown wings, and white bellies. The gray goslings nibble the grass and clover at their feet while their parents hover and stand guard. Tall and still, the parents watch the water rippling at their feet and the thick woods behind them for *predators* that might try to harm them. Luckily, the ocean is just a few yards away, and the geese can escape if a dog or fox decides to chase after them. If gulls or eagles swoop down to attack on the water, the geese can dive below the surface for safety.

A female Canada goose leads a family swim with her goslings and mate behind her. Canada geese mate for life and are devoted parents.

Geese have flat webbed feet to help them swim and powerful wings to help them fly.

But the seashore is quiet today, and the mother goose leads her goslings to the sandy shore and toward the lapping waves. One by one, the goslings follow her. Their father is at the end of the line, ready to protect his family. Soon the geese are out on the shimmering ocean and bobbing in the cool water. Their webbed feet are made for swimming.

Geese belong to the same family of *waterfowl* as ducks and swans. A waterfowl is a bird that swims. Geese, ducks, and swans can all swim, float, and dive below the surface of the water. Scientists call this family of waterfowl *Anatidae*. A female goose is called a goose, and a male goose is called a *gander*.

Geese have long necks, webbed feet to help them swim, and strong bills that can tear blades of grass or dig up roots of *aquatic* plants. Geese are larger than ducks but smaller than swans. A goose and a gander look very much alike, although the male is usually larger than the female.

Geese are birds. The scales on their legs and feet suggest that they are descended from reptilian-like ancestors. The oldest bird

Did You Know . . .
Several animals have the word goose in their names, but they are actually ducks. The pygmy goose, for example, is actually the world's smallest duck.

Archaeopteryx is the oldest known bird to have lived on earth. This creature was part reptile and its name means "ancient wing."

fossil belongs to Archaeopteryx, a creature that was part bird and part reptile and lived around 150 million years ago.

Like other birds, geese have powerful wings, and the bones on their legs, wings, and neck are hollow and light. Both flying and swimming are easy for them, but geese spend much of their time on land. There they peck away at grass and seeds with their bills and they use their *lamellae*—tiny, sharp ridges on their bills—to strain water from their food.

Because geese mainly eat grass, their bodies are designed to walk more easily on land than other waterfowl can. Their legs are placed at the center of their bodies rather than farther back like ducks or swans. Unlike ducks, geese do not waddle.

There are seven *species* of geese in the United States and Canada: Canada geese, white-fronted geese, snow geese, Ross's geese, brant geese, emperor geese, and Hawaiian geese.

With its black head, black neck, and white cheek feathers, the Canada goose is a familiar sight throughout North America. It is one of the most intelligent waterfowl. The Canada goose has excellent hearing and can even hear a nearby dog's tail wag!

Species Chart

◆ Canada geese have black heads and necks and a patch of white on their cheeks. These geese are found throughout North America and often build their nests in Canada. They fly north in large, noisy flocks to nest in the same places their parents did, although some geese stay where they are all year round. There are eleven kinds of Canada geese. With a wingspan of up to 6 feet (1.8 meters), the giant Canada goose, *Branta canadensis maxima*, is the largest goose in the world. It weighs up to 17 pounds (7.7 kilograms).

A Canada goose has a black head and neck and the famous white "chinstrap"—a patch of white feathers on its cheeks.

◆ The white-fronted goose is sometimes called the laughing goose. The noise it makes—ho leek leek—sounds like a hysterical laugh! This goose grows to be 26 to 31 inches (66 to 79 centimeters) long and weighs 4 to 7 pounds (1.8 to 3.2 kg). It has a white rump, orange legs, a black-speckled belly, and an orange or pink bill.

White-fronted geese stay with their parents longer than other geese. They will still be sharing a home next spring.

11

◆ The lesser snow goose is either all white or dark gray and brown. It has a white head, a pink bill, and rosy legs. This goose grows to be 27 to 33 inches (69 to 84 centimeters) long. It yelps like a fox terrier!

A lesser snow goose carefully watches over her gosling on its first swim.

◆ The Ross's goose is small and snowy white, with dark pink legs and black feathers at the tips of its wings. It can be 22 to 26 inches (56 to 66 cm) long, and it weighs about 3 to 4 pounds (1.4 to 1.8 kg). It nests in the Arctic but spends its winters mostly in California.

The Ross's goose has black tips on its white wing feathers.

2 Habitat and Features

Geese live in North America, Europe, and Asia—places in the Northern Hemisphere where they can find grass that is rich in protein. You will discover geese on grass and on ponds, lakes, rivers, marshes, and oceans—wide-open spaces where they can find food and stay protected. Geese tend to sleep on water with their heads tucked into their back feathers, away from predators such as coyotes and foxes.

Geese have a thick layer of *down* beneath their top layer of feathers. These soft, fluffy down feathers are waterproof and windproof, so they keep the goose warm. The goose's outer feathers are water-resistant as well.

Canada geese tuck in their bills and sleep on the water, safe from foxes, coyotes, and wolves.

Geese keep their feathers clean and in good condition. To bathe, geese dip their heads in water and shovel water over their backs. Then they reach back and use their *serrated* bills to comb their feathers into place. Geese produce an oil in a gland on top of their tails, and they spread this oil over their feathers to create a waterproof layer. The oil is so effective that water just rolls off! Feathers do wear out, though. Geese *molt*, or grow new body and tail feathers, once a year to replace worn ones.

Adult geese begin to shed their flight feathers during the summer. While they are molting, they cannot fly. For three to five weeks, the molting geese settle on a grassy feeding area where they can stay safe with a whole flock. Geese can fly again by early August, about six weeks after molting begins.

Geese are *vegetarians* that eat a variety of different foods. They nibble on short grasses and *sedges* as well as the roots, stems, leaves, and seeds of water plants. As geese look for food in the water, they point their tails up and duck their heads down as they reach for plants that grow at the bottom of the water.

Geese are vegetarians, and grass is one of their favorite foods.

Did You Know . . .
Most geese live in the wild, but there are some *domesticated* species that live on farms. Domesticated geese can lay up to 160 eggs a year. There is no chance that such geese will fly away. They are so well fed that their fat rear ends are too heavy to fly more than a foot in the air!

17

Canada geese dive below the surface of the water to feed on plants growing at the bottom of a pond.

18

Geese also eat seeds and grains. Kernels of dried corn are a favorite food. In Europe, the bean goose eats beans growing in the fields, as well as berries, flowers, and sunflower seeds.

Geese eat mainly during the day. If there is enough moonlight to keep an eye on predators, however, they will eat into the night. At least one goose watches out for the others and honks if it sees danger.

The Life Cycle of a Goose

Geese choose life mates when they are two or three years old. Females tend to lay their eggs near the nests where they hatched and flew for the first time. So year after year, geese return to the place where they first snuggled under their mothers' wings.

Canada geese are some of the first birds—and the first waterfowl—to build nests each spring. As warm spring air melts the last of the ice and snow, the geese mate on water. Then the females build their nests on dry land. Their nests must be near grass and water but safe from floods. The nesting sites also must allow the geese to see any foxes, wolves, skunks, coyotes, or polar bears that might sneak up and grab an egg or

This Canada goose will take good care of its gosling and teach it how to eat, swim, and fly.

The emperor goose likes to lay its eggs near water. When they are first laid, the emperor's eggs are pure white.

gosling. Small islands are perfect nesting sites because most land predators cannot reach them.

A mother goose gathers up twigs, small stones, and other materials for the nest. Then she softens the nest with weeds, grass, and moss. The goose even plucks a few of her own breast feathers to make a soft cushion.

The average goose lays four to seven eggs, or about one a day. The eggs are white or cream colored. The group of eggs is called a *clutch*. After all the eggs are laid, the mother goose gently sits down on them to *incubate*. This way she keeps them warm until they are ready to hatch.

If the goose needs to leave the nest to eat, drink, or take a bath, she covers the nest with a few feathers to hide the eggs and keep them warm. Her mate keeps an eye on her as she feeds, drinks, and bathes. If a predator approaches the mother goose or the nest, the gander will stand up tall, stretch out his neck, and hiss. He will chase after the intruder and attack it with his wings. Once the gander succeeds in driving the predator away, he will pump his head and neck up and down and honk loudly.

Did You Know . . .

When goslings are born, they do not know how to find food or to protect themselves. Their parents show them how to eat grass and hiss at enemies. The goslings stay with their parents for a full year. If their parents migrate, the goslings will travel south with them that fall and return to the very same nesting spot the following spring.

Goose eggs take about twenty-two to thirty days to hatch. When the eggs are ready, the goslings can be heard peeping and tapping against the inside of their shells. The goslings have a small egg tooth at the top of their bills. They use the tooth to peck away at the shell and free themselves. It can take a whole day for a gosling to hatch. When it does, it tumbles out headfirst with its eyes open. The little gosling is exhausted!

All the eggs hatch within a few hours of each other. The mother goose *broods* her babies. This means she

24

When they hatch, Canada geese are covered with fuzzy down feathers that are yellowish olive green.

By watching their parents, Canada geese learn how to find food and water, and how to flap their wings and fly. At eight or nine weeks, these young Canada geese will look like their parents and are ready to try to fly.

protects them and keeps them warm and safe beneath her wings. When they are first born, the goslings of Canada geese are soft, yellow-green balls. They have fuzzy down feathers. The color of the goslings' fuzz helps hide the little ones from predators. The goslings can also flatten themselves on the ground and blend into the grass so that hungry enemies cannot find them.

Several hours after the goslings hatch, their parents take them to the water, where they plop in for the first time. Their soft down feathers help them to float. The goslings can swim right away.

Back on land, the goslings tumble around their mother as she nibbles on grass, and start to eat themselves. Over the next two months, the young geese will grow new and stronger feathers to help them fly. Their wings will grow and develop, and their feathers will darken so they look more like adults. The goslings will test their wings and try to fly on land and on water. By the eighth or ninth week, the teenage goslings will look like their parents, and they will fly for the first time.

The young geese will need the ability to fly. Come fall, the grass and aquatic plants will die. The rivers and lakes where the geese drink and swim soon will be covered with ice and snow. With their food gone, the geese will need to move on. The young geese will gather in a *gaggle* in an open field with their parents, grandparents, aunts, uncles, and cousins. The geese will be well fed and ready for their epic journey south.

4 The Great Migration

Have you ever seen a flock of geese flying by in the autumn sky? The sound of hundreds of geese honking overhead is deafening, and the sight is unforgettable. Geese *migrate* to survive. The availability of food and the amount of daylight determine when geese migrate and to what place. When nights are longer and days are shorter, instinct tells the geese that it is time to leave for a warmer place.

Canada geese leave their summer homes in late summer or early fall. One bird—usually one of the older birds in the group, maybe a gander or a dominant female—takes the lead. It faces the wind and

Canada geese migrate to survive. They fly day and night with their families, stopping only briefly to eat and rest.

begins shaking its head and honking that it is time to go. Soon all the geese are off, following behind the lead bird. There might be thousands of birds darkening the sky as they fly off.

Geese fly in long lines in the shape of the letter V. This shape makes it easy for them to see and fly. The V-shaped form is called a *wedge* or *skein*. The lead bird flies headfirst into the wind. Gusts of wind may knock it around, but the birds in back of it have a much easier flight. The air rushing over the wings of the lead bird gives a little lift to the birds in back.

Thousands of Canada geese flock to their new winter home.

These Canada geese fly in a V-shaped pattern during a long migration. They travel the same route every year.

31

Geese are large, fast, and powerful fliers. They can fly over 40 miles (65 km) per hour. Migrating geese fly day and night. The birds in back honk to stay in touch with their leader, and they look out for danger while following familiar landmarks such as mountains or rivers. The younger geese learn the way on their first great journey.

Geese find their way year after year by using the sun. It helps them navigate because it shows which direction is north and south. Geese know that if they are flying south in the morning, the sun must be in the east, or to their left. The positions of the stars guide geese as well.

Some geese travel a long way during their migrations. If you see a V-shaped flock of geese, they are probably on a long trip—geese that fly just a short way are not as well organized. Some Canada geese do not travel very far, and some geese do not migrate at all. A black brant that spends its summers on the Alaskan peninsula will fly nearly 2,000 miles (3,200 km) over the Pacific Ocean to spend the winter in northern California. However, if Canada geese have enough food

Did You Know . . .
Geese fly very high in the sky. For example, a bar-headed goose flies as high as a passenger jet. Geese are distance fliers, too. Canada geese can fly as far as 650 miles (1,046 km) without stopping.

Upland geese like these live in South America and the Falkland Islands and do not migrate.

and water around their summer area, they might stay put. Their thick layer of down keeps them warm when winter arrives.

Migrating geese travel on four main routes. These migration *corridors* follow river valleys and seacoasts. The corridors are at most 10 miles (16 km) wide. Geese usually follow the same corridor every year because the route offers them plenty of places to eat and rest.

*These Canada geese
will be faithful
companions as long as
they both live.*

Geese usually make several stops along their migration, although some geese travel without stopping at all. A large group of snow geese, for example, flies 1,600 miles (2,574 km) nonstop from Hudson Bay in north-central Canada to marshes in Louisiana. When they do stop, geese often choose the same spots year after year.

Geese are faithful and devoted to each other along the migration route. If a goose disappears from the flock, its mate will leave the flock and honk. Hearing that familiar voice helps the lost goose find its way back to the flock.

If a goose is wounded or unable to fly, its mate might drop down and stay with it. Mating geese usually stay together while both are alive. If one mate dies, however, the surviving goose will look for a new mate before nesting season.

5 Protecting Geese

Geese can live in the wild for up to twenty years. They can chase away most predators, but they are not as successful at fending off humans. When workers drain wetlands to build shopping plazas and to pave parking lots, geese lose their nesting spots and homes. Hunting is deadly, too.

Hunting geese for food and sport has been popular for centuries, and roast goose is a favorite Christmas dish. In France, the fatty liver of domesticated ducks or geese is a prized food. People also use goose feathers to stuff pillows, warm winter jackets, hats, slippers, and quilts.

A crouching hunter, along with his eager dog, waits for the sound of a goose.

By the late 1800s, hunting geese for food and feathers had taken its toll on wild populations. In 1918, the United States signed the Migratory Bird Treaty Act. That law made rules to protect migratory birds, their nests, and their eggs.

The Migratory Bird Treaty Act came just in time for the nene goose, a small brown goose that lives in Hawaii and is the Hawaiian state bird. Hunters, poachers, and egg collectors nearly wiped out the nene back in the early 1900s. By 1918 there were only about thirty left. Today, the Audubon Society estimates there are 1,700 surviving nene geese. The bird is still protected by the Endangered Species Act.

The director of the U.S. Fish and Wildlife Service decides when to place an animal or plant on the federal endangered species list. The U.S. Department of the Interior—a government agency that oversees the U.S. Fish and Wildlife Service—decides which migratory birds may be hunted, if any. Because the nene goose is on the endangered list, it cannot be hunted.

In 1967, the Aleutian Canada goose was placed on the endangered list. This goose

Did You Know . . .

The red-breasted goose builds its nest within a few feet of the nest of a peregrine falcon. The goose and its eggs stay safe because no animal dares to come near the falcon, with its hooked beak and sharp claws!

The nene goose is an endangered bird that is found only on the islands of Hawaii.

builds its nests in the Aleutian Islands. So many Aleutian Canada geese were eaten by arctic and red foxes that in 1975 there were only about 790. Biologists carefully moved some of the geese onto a fox-free island where they could graze and nest in peace, and the scientists continued to transplant geese over the next twenty years. Biologists also removed foxes from thirty-five other islands. All of the conservation efforts were so successful that the goose was removed from the endangered species list in 2001.

The government has been so successful at protecting Canada geese that U.S. officials now have a different problem—too many Canada geese! According to the U.S. Fish and Wildlife Service, the geese produce so many babies that the population can double

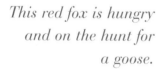

This red fox is hungry and on the hunt for a goose.

A pair of Canada geese and their young goslings are a happy sight each spring.

every five or six years. Also, a Canada goose can create a pound or more of waste every day. The waste pollutes ponds, streams, and reservoirs. Geese are sometimes hurtful to farms, too, because they eat grain, trample soil, and ruin crops.

Canada geese may create some problems, but other geese, such as the nene, need our protection. One of the U.S. Fish and Wildlife Service's goals is to make sure people will be able to enjoy wild geese and other waterfowl for many years to come. For example, a blue goose is the symbol of the National Wildlife Refuge System logo. As geese walk through our parks and yards, they put us in touch with wildlife close to home. Hearing their honking in the skies overhead is truly a sign of fall and spring.

Glossary

Anatidae—A family of swimming birds that includes geese, ducks, and swans.

aquatic—Growing in, on, or near water.

brood—To protect baby birds by covering them with wings.

clutch—A group of bird's eggs that are laid by the same mother during one season.

corridors—The routes that migrating geese follow between their winter and summer homes.

domesticated—Suitable for living and working with humans.

down—An underlayer of soft, fluffy feathers.

gaggle—A group of geese.

gander—A male goose.

goslings—Baby geese.

incubate—To keep eggs warm so that the babies inside will develop and hatch.

lamellae—Tiny comblike ridges or teeth inside the bills of geese and other waterbirds used to drain water from food and to clean feathers.

migrate—To travel from one place to another in a seasonal pattern.

molt—To shed feathers and grow new ones.

predators—Animals that hunt other animals for food.

sedges—Grasslike plants that grow in wet places.

serrated—Having teeth like a saw.

skein—A flock of geese or similar birds in the sky.

species—Groups of animals or plants that are very much alike and can mate with other members of the same species.

vegetarians—Living things that eat only plants.

waterfowl—Swimming birds that spend a long time living on water.

wedge—A V-shaped flock of birds.

Find Out More

Books

Bradley, James V. *The Canada Goose.* New York: Chelsea House Publications, 2006.

Johnson, Jinny. *1000 Things You Should Know About Birds.* Essex, United Kingdom: Miles Kelly Publishing Ltd., 2008.

Winner, Cherie. *Everything Bird: What Kids Really Want to Know About Birds.* Minnetonka, MN: NorthWord Books for Young Readers, 2007.

Websites

Audubon Society
www.audubon.org

National Geographic: Canada Geese
http://kids.nationalgeographic.com/Animals/
CreatureFeature/Canadagoose

National Wildlife Federation
www.nwf.org

U.S. Fish & Wildlife Service: Educating for
Conservation
www.fws.gov/educators/students.html

Wisconsin Department of Natural
Resources: Canada Goose
www.dnr.state.wi.us/eek/critter/bird/
goose.htm

World Wildlife Fund
www.worldwildlife.org

Index

Page numbers for illustrations are in **boldface**.

About the Author

Darice Bailer has written more than two dozen children's books. She won Parents' Choice Gold Awards for a book on puffins and a book on humpback whales. Bailer has been a freelance journalist for many years, and her articles have appeared in *The New York Times*. She lives with her family in Connecticut.